EIGHT
HABITS
OF
THE
HEART

John Dieckman

Our shared
Lives

Clg Taulbert
8/27/99

Also by Clifton L. Taulbert

WHEN WE WERE COLORED

THE LAST TRAIN NORTH

WATCHING OUR CROPS COME IN

EIGHT HABITS OF THE HEART

The Timeless Values That

Build Strong Communities—

Within Our Homes and Our Lives

CLIFTON L. TAULBERT

Viking / Dial Books

VIKING / DIAL BOOKS
Published by the Penguin Group
Penguin Putnam Inc., 375 Hudson Street, New York, New York 10014, U.S.A.
Penguin Books Ltd, 27 Wrights Lane, London W8 5TZ, England
Penguin Books Australia Ltd, Ringwood, Victoria, Australia
Penguin Books Canada Ltd, 10 Alcorn Avenue,
Toronto, Ontario, Canada M4V 3B2
Penguin Books (N.Z.) Ltd, 182–190 Wairau Road,
Auckland 10, New Zealand

Penguin Books Ltd, Registered Offices: Harmondsworth, Middlesex, England

First published in 1997 by Viking Penguin
and Dial Books, members of Penguin Putnam Inc.

1 3 5 7 9 10 8 6 4 2

LIBRARY OF CONGRESS CATALOGING IN PUBLICATION DATA
Taulbert, Clifton L.
Eight habits of the heart : the timeless values that build strong
communities—within our homes and our lives / Clifton L. Taulbert
p.   cm.
ISBN 0-670-87545-7
1. Afro-Americans—Mississippi—Glen Allan—Social life and
customs.   2. Afro-Americans—Mississippi—Glen Allan—Conduct of
life.   3. Conduct of life.   4. Glen Allan (Miss.)—Social life and
customs.   5. Taulbert, Clifton L.—Childhood and youth.
6. Glen Allan (Miss.)—Biography.   I. Title.
F349.G54T37   1997
976.2'42—dc21   97–4230

This book is printed on acid-free paper.

Printed in the United States of America
Set in Cloister
DESIGNED BY BRIAN MULLIGAN

This book is dedicated to the youth who will build community for their generation, to those who are building community today, and to the former generations who showed us how.

CONTENTS

ACKNOWLEDGMENTS

I want to thank three special friends for encouraging me to write this book and helping me to shape and title it: Charlotte Stewart, Vicki Lake, and Dr. Delores Saunders. I want also to thank Kevin Randolph, Paul Perkinson, John Knight, and Julie Hall, the head of the North Shore Country Day School, for providing the wonderful graduates who caused me to focus on the gifts my people had given me and gave me the opportunity to pass them along.

A special thanks also to my wife, Barbara, and son, Marshall, for keeping me attuned to my need to practice these habits at home. And to our darling daughter, Anne Kathryn, who during her short seven years of life gave us the opportunity to live these ideals in front of her, ideals that I know she would want us to pass along.

EIGHT HABITS OF THE HEART

PREFACE

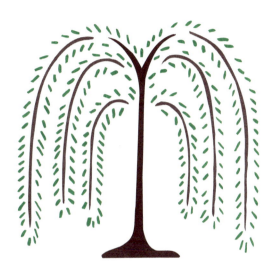

Shaping the Gift

They were my benefactors and I was their heir, but they had no stocks or bonds to give me. My parents, relatives, and neighbors simply gave me the best of what they had. Although they lived behind a wall called "legal segregation," they ignored its boundaries when it came to nurturing their children. Instead, gathering us together on their porches, which were their principal meeting places, they set out to shield us from segregation's woes by building a good community for our dreams. They, the "porch people" of the Mississippi Delta, knew how to build such community because their parents had built community for them.

Today, looking back, I call their community-building practices Eight Habits of the Heart—habits that I sought to describe for the 1995 graduating class of the North Shore Country Day School in the Chicago suburb of Winnetka, Illinois, when they invited me to speak at their commencement. This book grew out of that speech, and out of my rich remembering.

In the fall of 1994 I had been startled and pleased to receive a call from Julie Hall, head of this well-known private high school. Their senior class had been introduced to my writings two years before by Kevin Randolph, a member of the faculty, and now they were asking me to address their seventy-fifth graduating class the following May.

I was honored that these students had selected me. I knew they were a group of America's brightest young people, for I had been conducting a dialogue with them for some time. After reading my first book, a memoir of my growing-up years called *When We Were Colored*, they had written me to ask questions about what it was like to come of age during the era of legal segregation in the Mississippi Delta. Although I was unable to answer each letter, I did collect all of their questions and answer them in one letter to the class. Thus began a relationship that culminated in my becoming their commencement speaker.

However, as I began to contemplate their invitation, I wondered what of value I could tell these students, many of whom had come from homes and families comfortable enough to make important dreams come true. I had achieved some degree of international acceptance as a businessman and then as a writer. But theirs was a school that had produced many notable alumni—individuals like internationally acclaimed cellist Wendy Warner; the developer of time-lapse photography, John Nash Ott, Jr.; computer pioneer Edward L. (Ted) Glaser; and the first woman to serve as chief of neurology at a U.S. teaching hospital, Dr. Anne B. Young, who practices at Massachusetts General.

Nevertheless, I was the one they had asked to speak, and as I thought about what I might say, my thoughts went back to my own elementary and secondary school graduations. Both were so special, but my eighth-grade graduation from Moore's Elementary School was especially memorable because my great-grandfather, Poppa Joe Young, gave the commencement speech. I had lived with him and my great-grandmother, Mama Pearl, when I was small.

On my graduation day we were all excited. Poppa's stepdaughter, Ma Ponk—my great-aunt, with whom I had lived since I was six—had pressed her hair, something she did only for the best occasions. It was a grand event, and I was at its center. Moreover, Poppa Joe, who was a Southern Baptist preacher, knew exactly what to say; and on that special day his carefully chosen words and thunderous voice helped me see that I would encounter a series of futures in my life, the first of which began that day, with my departure from Moore's Elementary School. O'Bannon High School in Greenville, to which our little class would go, was only twenty-eight miles away, but Poppa made it sound like a journey to the stars. And for many of us, it was.

But what about the graduates at North Shore Country Day School? Their lives had been so different from mine, and surely many of them already had the means to "journey to the stars." Still, there was something about the life I had lived as a child, as described in my book, that had captivated them.

I thought of great quotes that I might use from distinguished writers, preachers, and politicians. But I wanted to give the students a speech from the heart, one whose message they could embrace now and still remember some thirty years later, just as I could still remember Poppa's charge to me and my eighth-grade classmates: to do our best, mind our manners, think of others, and make our families proud as we marched into our future.

The more I thought, the more I realized that I had to find a way to draw my own picture for the students, a picture of what I knew was of value to me. How, I wondered, could I manage to give them what my people had given me? Would I be able to capture the conversations of maids, field workers, old preachers, teachers, and tractor drivers, and do their lives justice before the students, faculty, and parents I would find at this sophisticated school?

Of course! As characters in my books, the porch people had fared well, and kindred spirits had recognized their extraordinary qualities as human beings. Just as their stories had brought great joy to my Cousin Savannah back home, they had also deeply affected people as far away as South Africa, where members of that country's parliament had read them. And in numerous talks, I had credited my elders with providing the foundation for my success. From my days in college and graduate school through my later years with my marketing firm and my writing, I knew who was responsible for my achievements—the people back home. Now I was determined to rise to the challenge of presenting their lives, their virtues, and their truths as a gift to others.

And so I slipped back to the porches of Glen Allan, Mississippi, to the memories that had served me well, to begin shaping a gift worth giving. As I drafted my speech, I began to key in on words that wouldn't let go, words that focused my attention on the graveled road I knew so well. I remembered Preacher Hurn, the man we called the "ole African," and how he would come into Glen Allan from the colored colony where he lived. He just walked the streets, speaking with a stutter, but always compelling as he admonished parents to watch their children, whom he found to be "marked for good." As I recollected the unvarying but heartening message of Preacher Hurn, I suddenly thought, It was a habit. He did it all the time! And what a habit it was, now that I remembered it. The whole town must have been addicted, because most of them had similar habits.

I knew what a habit was—it was something you couldn't help doing. But the kind of habit I was thinking of came not from drugs or liquid spirits but from the commitment of human hearts. So I began toying with the words "habit" and "heart" to describe my legacy from the porch people of Glen Allan. I finally hit upon "Habits of the Heart," a concept I thought to be uniquely mine until further study revealed that the nineteenth-century French author Alexis de Tocqueville had also used this expression when writing about America in the 1830's. Perhaps I had heard the phrase before, in my history classes in college, and had forgotten it. Nevertheless, even if the term was not original with me, the people who practiced such habits during my childhood were uniquely mine. I liked the term, I thought it suited them well, and I was sure it had just as much significance for me as it had had for de Tocqueville over a century before.

I was pleased to put my people in his company. As a child I had drawn from them a sense of worth that was often unacknowledged by a segregated world. They had taken my kinship to slaves and made me proud that I was a survivor, with new worlds to conquer. And when I asked myself who I was, the community of family and friends was there to answer. They told me that I was good and that my life had value.

As I contemplated what my elders had done for me, I identified the eight ideals they had passed on to me— nurturing attitude, dependability and responsibility, friendship, brotherhood, high expectations, courage, and hope—Eight Habits of the Heart. And so I built my speech on these, making every effort to convey their value by describing the community built by the people who had practiced them daily.

That speech was the beginning of this book, which gradually formed in the months that followed as audiences around the United States and the world listened to me elaborate upon the Eight Habits of the Heart. Soon after I left Illinois, I went to Nashville, Tennessee, to give the keynote address at the prestigious "Future 50" banquet of the Nashville Chamber of Commerce, honoring that city's top fifty emerging businesses. I told this audience of business and civic leaders about the relevance of the Habits of the Heart to good business, good relationships, and community connections—and the response was overwhelming.

At the end of the speech, in which I introduced the humble folk of the Mississippi Delta to a mostly white, successful audience, nearly everyone asked me to give them a list of the habits and tell them where they might find my comments in print. On the next day I was further assured that Poppa's good practices had hit home when the *Nashville Banner*'s business page bore the headline: "'Future 50' speaker stresses 'Habits of the Heart.'"

From Nashville I traveled to Frankfurt, Germany, where I spoke to an international meeting of over three hundred educators who had come from throughout Europe and from as far away as Panama. Again I chose to share with this group the community-building importance of the Habits of the Heart to their educational purposes and professional lives, and again the audience asked if this material was written down.

Later, in Tokyo, Japan, I spoke to a much smaller international group whose members were part of a program designed to strengthen the bonds between educators and parents. I applied the Eight Habits of the Heart to their endeavor, giving examples of how these habits were lived out by people who should have been bitter and angry but instead had built a strong community behind the wall of legal segregation. I especially shared my memories of Mama Pearl and my first day at school, and of the relationship that existed between her and my teacher, Miss Maxey. It was as if they planned together on a regular basis how to get the best out of me. At the end of the day a lady from Sri Lanka came up to me and said, "Our worlds were so different, but your world today has touched my heart."

Gratified and challenged by these responses from very different parts of the world, I realized that I had to write down the basic values of my community so I could share them with an even larger audience. Thus came this book, *Eight Habits of the Heart,* which I hope will serve as a catalyst for community-building for people everywhere.

THE
FIRST HABIT
OF THE HEART:
NURTURING
ATTITUDE

*In the community, a nurturing attitude
is characterized by unselfish caring,
supportiveness, and a willingness
to share time.*

Looking into the face of my son and his friends, I can see the future, a future as bright as the gifts and talents they bring to it. Yet their future is also heavily burdened with problems that stem from the breakdown of families and the lack of remembered community in the world outside their school walls. The media remind us of this daily. People are hurting, both here and around the globe. We hear the cries and imagine the pain. Nevertheless, we are challenged to look within ourselves to create for our children the best of what was provided to us.

Many of us remember a time when our lives and the success of our lives were the concerns of a great number of people, not just our primary families. I too recall such a time, which amazingly took place during legal segregation, when the elders of my community were often relegated to an inferior role. Yet in spite of that, they managed to create a nurturing environment that beckoned me to the future and continues to play a key role in my life. This is how a nurturing attitude looked and felt in my small Mississippi Delta town when I first became the beneficiary of this habit of the heart.

Poppa Joe Young's frame house was a grand place to a little boy like me. It had been built at the turn of the century by my maternal great-great-grandfather, Sidney Peters. Grandfather Peters had died long before I was born, but the house and the long front porch with its tall steps were still there, waiting for me to come along. While I enjoyed sitting on the steps in those early years when I lived with Poppa and Mama Pearl, I often climbed up onto the porch and sat at Poppa's feet as he entertained his friends. Because I was a child, I didn't say much, but I recall how the old men would come and spend a large part of the afternoon laughing, talking, and discussing the great drama of life. Of course, Mama Pearl was always there with southern sweets—like her red jelly cake, a yellow layer cake with jelly filling whipped up for an everyday dessert—and I watched as they ate together and shared their dreams.

The sick were always discussed. And Poppa made sure that someone was appointed to look in on them. If somebody was critically ill, they would all chip in and pay the Sister Workers Society dues, an assessment that served as an insurance policy. That was a must. No one wanted to be embarrassed at death. "Now, Elder, you take care of yourself" echoed from the steps, after their talking was over and they prepared to leave. Poppa always wished the old men well, and they often patted me on the head as they walked down the steps out to the old graveled road that would take them home.

Even though they were adults with an established routine, I was not overlooked by my great-grandparents and their friends. Poppa always smiled at me in a way that told me everything was right with the world. It didn't matter that laborious field work was these people's lot. Time was found to make me laugh and feel important.

Interwoven between long days in the field and equally long nights at church revival meetings were trips I made with Poppa to Greenville and to Hollandale, our "big cities." Though I liked Greenville best, I was just as delighted to go to Hollandale, where Cousin Sarah lived.

Poppa always visited Cousin Sarah when we went to Hollandale. She lived alone after her daughter grew up and moved to St. Louis. Sarah was family, and even though she and Cousin Saul Peters had divorced many years before, she never lost her place with us. A short woman, with black skin as smooth as a new onion, she always welcomed us and we always came.

Although Cousin Sarah lived in Hollandale, she belonged to the Sister Workers Society in Glen Allan, and Poppa picked up her dues as well as the news. She had a swing on the front porch where she'd sit for her visit with Poppa, who was always given a good chair. Because I was little, I would sit on the front steps, but I was neverthe-less part of the life they lived in front of me.

Cousin Sarah's kitchen held things we didn't often get to eat—tempting leftovers from Dr. Jack's house, where she worked as a cook. She was proud of her job and we were all proud of her fancy dishes, which she often shared with us as we sat on her front porch. She knew that I liked lemon pie, and whenever I came, she al-ways managed to find a piece just big enough for me. Poppa preferred her sweet potato pie, which was always there for him, along with a cup of good hot coffee. As we ate, they talked, and for a while the lady was not alone but part of the family she loved. As they sat discussing the condition of our kin, their faces by turns would re-flect the lights and shadows of concern and joy.

Cousin Sarah had been a single mother for years and was proud of her pretty daughter, my cousin Annette. But she worried about her grandchildren growing up in the city. So in the summer, when they came to stay with her for a while, she would teach them the same types of lessons that Poppa and Mama Pearl were teaching me. Although her world was not all she wished it to be, she never let go of her deep family ties. There were always visits to be paid and food to be shared. And families today, no matter who or where they are, still need to tend to each other and share their lives in those ways.

Talking across the back fences was also a way of life for the adults I knew. At home in Glen Allan we had three gardens and four fences to talk across. Uncle Abe Brown's house was on the west and our front gardens were side by side, separated by a wire mesh fence that had already seen its best days. Both Poppa Joe and Uncle Abe worked their gardens as energetically as they did the fields that provided their livelihood. However, across the fence they threw "care and concern" back and forth as they worked to raise a good stand of vegetables.

Uncle Abe Brown was also our justice of the peace and married many of Glen Allan's colored couples in his front room. My elders believed in marriage and the value of bringing up a family. Oftentimes Uncle Abe and Poppa would discuss a young couple's decision to tie the knot. I listened and didn't understand much of what they said, but I remember how they leaned into the fence and talked, sharing wisdom they had stored up over the years. And on occasions when Poppa was unable to deliver the covenant—religious sacraments—to an ailing church member, Uncle Abe could always be counted on to help. They were neighbors, and I saw them respect and care for each other.

Mr. Charlie Burkes's garden backed up to Poppa's

potato truck patch, a small garden where only one veg-
etable was grown. And Mr. Jim Morris's fence separated
Poppa's corn from the Morrises' yard. On many days all
the gardens were abuzz with conversation. Home reme-
dies were shared. They seemed always to be looking for a
new way to rid their houses of "the pleurisy." And if they
weren't discussing an endless case of the flu, they were
talking about who had "sugar." It was a long time before
I realized that the sugar of which they spoke was not
sweet or edible but was a deadly disease called diabetes.

Dreams were born across those mesh fences as the
neighbors talked proudly about children who had gone
off to college or into military service. And every thread
of social change was discussed as they wove for me a picture of the future.

Most of the time I just tagged along after Poppa, bare-
foot and bare chested, following his instructions when I
was not getting in his way. Poppa enjoyed my company,
and I liked being there. I was home.

Although I had never met my natural father, I was
surrounded by role models who gave me all the life instructions I would ever need. And those same kinds of
actions and instructions are still needed by children
growing up in every kind of home. Life doesn't have to
be perfect for adults to keep company with their young.

Even when I was so small that Poppa was still setting
me up on an Orange Crush soda crate placed on the seat

of a chair to get my hair cut, I knew that there was more to Glen Allan than Poppa's house. There were friends and family throughout the colored community. A few of our friends lived almost uptown in a small area that we called "the quarters." I don't know how it got such a name, but the houses there had only two rooms each, and they were built so close together that their porches almost touched. Conversations were never private, but laughter was contagious and sadness was felt by all. Mr. Clarence Hall, Sr., his daughter, Rosie May, my paternal great-grandparents, Mr. Eddie and his wife, Miss Addie, and my godparents, Mr. Cape and Miss Bessie Ann, all lived together in the tiny row of houses. The cool evenings and the weekends would bring them out to the porches where food was shared, jokes were told, and hair was cut. They all shared a single outdoor toilet and grew their small gardens out back. They watched out for each other, guarded their meager property, and kept a protective eye on us children as we passed.

Many times family and friends who lived on the small plantations that sat outside of Glen Allan proper would walk to town, and the quarters would always be the first colored houses they encountered. In the quarters a place to rest was always available. Water fountains were not common and uptown restaurants were closed to us, but not the quarters. The tired could stop, use the outdoor toilet, rest their feet, and get a drink of water. That's the way it was. I never knew it to be any different. And on Sunday mornings the blacktopped road was filled as the colored people from the quarters spilled out into the streets on their way to church. Though they went to different churches, they walked and shared time together. Poppa taught me to know and respect them all, and they knew me.

Most of the adults I knew lived their lives in such a way that we as children sensed their unity—a necessity, if they were to provide a caring and supportive environment for their children. Today I call their collective activity "nurturing attitude," but they never heard such a term. They never defined their actions, they just did what they knew was right to do. I know that the gardens I enjoyed can't be re-created, nor will I ever return to the front porch I knew as a child, but that heartfelt commitment to my well-being still challenges me to provide the same kind of nurture for the youth I encounter, and to practice it among the adults I know.

We must strive to practice this "nurturing attitude" despite the obstacles we face. Certainly there were obstacles in Glen Allan when I was young. Legal segregation, racism, and poverty marked our lives, but they were never pervasive enough to keep my elders from doing what was right. Although our country has made great strides since then, our communities still face hardships—some new, some left over from the past. As the cost of living rises, families run faster, harder, and longer just to keep up, and in the process run away from each other and themselves; children carry guns to school; drugs spawn violence and despair; and the rhetoric of intolerance flashes like lightning across our land, dimming our best dreams.

Each problem cries out for us to practice what my elders knew—this first habit of the heart, a nurturing attitude. When I was a young man, I thought I'd be young forever and that my elders would always be there for me. Life changed and it happened with such subtlety that before I knew it I had become a man, striving to be a community-builder myself.

In our worlds, wherever we are, the opportunity to build a good community is there. From the classroom to the sports field to the office cubicle, there are people who wait to hear someone say "welcome." No one really enjoys always eating alone or having no one to talk with. We were given time so it can be shared with others. I saw the old folk share their time and the joy of life that resulted.

No matter what age we are, or where we are, we need

to take this basic value and make it a habit of the heart. We need to practice it whenever and wherever we can. Extol it and praise it. Tuck it under jerseys, hum it during breaks, pack it in our new briefcases, practice it with strangers as well as friends. A nurturing attitude is a critical asset in the building of community, and, for every generation, a necessary habit of the heart.

THE SECOND
AND THIRD HABITS
OF THE HEART:

DEPENDABILITY
AND
RESPONSIBILITY

Within the community, dependability is being there for others through all the times of their lives, a steady influence that makes tomorrow a welcome event; and responsibility means showing and encouraging a personal commitment to each task.

The next two habits of the heart are those of dependability and responsibility. While previous generations took it for granted that these habits were worth cultivating, in many places they have all but disappeared—and community has vanished with them. Yet as a child I saw these habits practiced in my small town; I took the memory of what I saw north when I first left my Mississippi Delta home in 1963, and that memory remains with me to this day.

Had my own elders not been dependable and responsible in their dealings with each other, I would not have had a safe world in which to dream. In Glen Allan, they called it your "good word." "No need to trouble yourself," they would say. "You can count on me." These phrases were repeated over and over in conversations I overheard and actions I observed. This is how dependability and responsibility looked in a small southern town.

"Brother Cleve will be here at nine o'clock. He ain't never late,"

Ma Ponk said as she got me ready to join her for a ride to the country to see her sister, Aunt Willie Mae. Even if I wanted to slow the process, I was too small to have such power, so I just let my body go limp while Ma Ponk overdressed me. Uncle Cleve was the iceman, and it was said you could set your clock by his schedule, which never changed.

In their colored world of uncertain futures, both dependability and responsibility were necessary. After all, we lived under a system that should have provided us with good schools and new books but didn't, that kept industries with high ethical standards from coming into our area, and that made sure favors were handed out only to the socially and politically compliant. And when the system and all else failed—the job, the boss, and even the law—the people were left with each other and the routines they had established, which embraced both the secular and the sacred.

There were no contracts to guarantee their actions, just their words and the memory of the traditions they upheld. Even our school janitors were part of the tradition of dependability and responsibility, working with our teachers and our parents to make the school a showplace. It didn't matter what "rights" had been denied the colored school in the courts; the schoolyard was still trimmed like carpet and the tile floors reflected our faces. Mr. Powell, our janitor, had a responsibility that was more important than the legal system that slighted our world and had overlooked him. Outside our community he may have been called "the cleaning man," but he was more than a janitor; he was part of that benevolent conspiracy that existed among the adults to make our educational experience memorable. And it was. Day after day our principal depended upon Mr. Powell to make our school a special place, and Mr. Powell never let us down.

As I think back, you could actually tuck the word of these dependable people under your pillow and proceed with the rest of your life. In addition to Mr. Powell, there was Miss Carrie, our school cook, who lived in Alps, a small cotton community right outside Glen Allan. Many parents who rose before dawn to work in the fields did well just to get their children off to school, let alone prepare them healthy, hearty breakfasts. However, the study and work we children faced at school was brightened by the knowledge that at noon we would be invited into Miss Carrie's world, where good hot food would be waiting.

No matter how hard it rained or how low our supplies might get, Miss Carrie was always there to feed us; and each day she bade us good-bye with these same words: "See you tomorrow, children." Dressed in white, with wire-rimmed glasses, and graying hair tucked under a net, Miss Carrie held a position of authority and respect. And she never let anything keep her from her work.

I don't know how our elders did it. They never

seemed to retire. The fields were their factories, plants, and offices. They had to take care of the family, to provide food, housing, and clothes. Their means of earning money were few, usually backbreaking field work and other jobs that could be demeaning. But they didn't stop. So much depended on the circulation of their small incomes, but they were good for their part. Today when I sometimes grow tired of writing, editing, and rewriting, I am reminded that this is my job, a job that is connected to the hopes and aspirations of other people. I am also reminded that being responsible is what my people taught me, and any abdication of that responsibility has consequences that reach far beyond myself.

In my small town the older people were to us the sun and the moon. We rose to face the day because they did it before us. We welcomed the night because they said it always came. And when we found ourselves overwhelmed by the harsh reality of the day, they were there to shore up our spirits and keep us looking to the future. For me the habits of responsibility and dependability became people, not just wishful thoughts, but living, breathing people who placed my welfare in the center of their lives.

When I am asked to picture dependability and responsibility, I find it easy to do. I just go back to the small white frame house where I grew up after Mama Pearl got sick and she and Poppa Joe couldn't keep me anymore. It was Ma Ponk's house from which I left for school each day. And that was no small task. The system was segregated and I had to go to Greenville to school. It was twenty-eight miles away but much longer when you added in the miles we detoured to pick up the kids from the various Delta plantations, which made the trip almost fifty miles there and fifty miles back.

So I had to get up early. The bus driver, Murray Washington, had to get up even earlier, as did Ma Ponk, who would stand on the front porch and flip the lights on and off, so that the driver would know I was going that day. No matter what, Mr. Murray never missed a day, and Ma Ponk never missed a flip.

Even today I still see Ma Ponk standing on the front porch, her scarf tied tightly around her head with her flannel gown wrapped around her failing frame. She was always there and Mr. Murray always came. On such faithfulness is good community built. So many adults took seriously their roles in our lives that generations of young "colored" kids worked their way around and through the barriers of racism and bigotry to become major partners in the shaping of America.

Ma Ponk raised me in the role of a single parent, but she didn't do it alone. Today, when so many families are headed by single parents, a responsible and dependable community is all the more essential. Nor can two-parent families do it all. Although I value the opportunity to rear my son and pass along to him much of what was given me, I also know that part of his rearing will take place outside of my watch.

Much has changed since I was a child, but the need for all people—regardless of their circumstances—to accept responsibility and practice dependability has not changed. After all, here on the edge of the twenty-first century we still face a vast array of challenges to community that cannot be overcome by technological innovations. Even the Internet, which facilitates communication of all kinds, can be used either as a bridge that brings us together or as a weapon that tears us apart. And although advances in the fields of medicine and public health have also made life easier in many respects, they can neither create community nor make up for its absence. In a world where progress is measured in bits and bytes, advanced technology will never be able to replace the need for good minds, strong wills, and unselfish hearts.

Though my examples were from the Delta, the habits of dependability and responsibility are found in strong communities around the world. I have tried to show how these habits looked when I was young. The look hasn't changed.

THE
FOURTH HABIT
OF THE HEART:
FRIENDSHIP

*Within the community, friendship is the
habit that binds people together when they
take pleasure in each other's company,
listen, laugh, and share
good times and bad.*

True friendship can form bridges between people that last all their lives. But when friendship is absent, people often live in envy and fear, and community breaks down. True friendship goes beyond easy banter and jokes. It encircles people with laughter but also helps them embrace others in the midst of their own pain. It was on the strength of this kind of friendship, the next habit of the heart, that the elders who reared me and secured my future also built community.

In those days it seemed as if every southern kitchen had at least one big iron pot. Such pots were always boiling, always sending savory smells throughout the house. I remember the feeling of warmth and welcome that emanated from the small kitchens of our community as the sounds of cooking drew us closer to the source of the smells. Many times we had no idea what was cooking and we were told, "Never lift the top!" The heavy tops were as formidable as the watchful eyes of our grandmothers. They stayed put, no matter how much we wanted to lift them. They held in the flavors that made the food taste good—the green beans, corn, rice, neck bones, pepper, salt, and secret stuff all mingling together over the fire.

The friendships I encountered growing up kept everything together, much like those heavy tops. They held in the flavors of our lives in spite of all the challenges that a legally segregated society produced, and they caused our laughter, our cares, our joy, and our dreams to mingle and be shared.

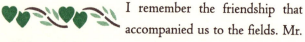 I remember the friendship that accompanied us to the fields. Mr. Walter's field truck came early, even before the sun awakened in the Delta, and we would sleepily rub our eyes as we climbed in the back. But how quickly the atmosphere changed as the truck gathered more and more people. Sleepy eyes soon opened wide as all kinds of secrets were shared. The sound of laughter woke us up as conversation from the newcomers made its way into our midst. And we were packed so close together that the laughter of one became the laughter of us all.

Whether Saturday night juke joint news or Sunday morning repentance, we heard it all in the fields. Miss Honey Pie always had the best news, the news I should not have heard—messages from the adult world that generated knowing laughter, slaps on the knees, and heavy pats on the back. Everybody knew Honey Pie, whom they called "the prettiest black lady in the world." Her skin was midnight black with a fine velvet glow. Her teeth were like ivory and glistened when she smiled. Even though I was just a boy, I knew she was well shaped. On her frequent walks into town from Linden Plantation, where she lived, her hips would sway—and everybody watched. With her sweet way she could have had almost any man, and she chose Cooter Man, who watched every move she made. She was his lady, but we all shared her warmth.

Honey Pie was a fun-filled woman, and it was her memory of Saturday night that we wanted to hear. When Cooter Man was away driving tractors, she would become our radio. We hung on to her every word and eagerly awaited her contagious laugh. Her friendship kept us going and raised our spirits up. Her stories lifted us off the bed of Mr. Walter's truck and into her world of nighttime escapades, and we laughed and laughed as we rolled on toward the fields. It was that world of friends that got us through the day as the sun came up and began to pound the Delta with heat. All morning as we picked, sweat poured from our brows like rain.

When we stopped for lunch, the older people would be helped to the best seats on the bed of the truck to rest, while the young ones sat beneath the truck or found the shade of a rare tree. Leftover fried chicken, cold baked sweet potatoes, Moon Pies, pork and beans, and canned sardines with crackers would be passed around, and we swapped stories and retold our dreams. Everyone was "Cuz" and the old people were "Miss" and "Mister" in this world of ordinary people who made memories that would last me all my life.

The hot Delta fields may seem an unlikely place for friendship to flourish, but flourish it did. It was the power of friendship that blocked out the hurt, the ache, and the pain of the backbreaking work that was our way of life. There never seemed to be trees, just miles and miles of flat land and endless cotton rows, shimmering in the heat. Yet I remember all of us piling off the truck, heading to the fields, taking our laughter with us—and our songs.

I am convinced that the "blues" were born in the fields, not on a sweaty night in a shotgun house. From way across the field, coming up from the stalks of cotton, you could hear the slow moaning sound of a great singer, probably never to be discovered except by us. Singing was just as much a part of the cotton scene as the work itself. It distanced us from the rigors of the job, and when a good singer struck out by himself we'd all quiet down to listen. A low melodious moaning seemed to rise up from the earth, and as the sound got louder, we waited for some words to ring out too: drawn-out melodies of hurting, and how "you done me wrong." The blues. Some would join in with backup in a field-style harmony. The song would be good, although we'd probably never hear it on a jukebox. But it didn't matter. We loved the song, and we would cheer the singer on. And if he seemed to miss a note, we told him. After all, we knew good singing when we heard it.

Backs were bent, but voices were lifted. The days were long, but the friendship was longer. Day in and day out, laughter continued and friendship grew, even in the midst of a world that hadn't planned on our survival. Laughter healed the hurt and the blues bound up the bruise.

I also saw friendship driving down our small, partially paved road in a shiny black Model T Ford, which belonged to Mr. and Mrs. George Stanley. They were old lovers who were also the best of friends, and their "friendship" was special when you consider the world they knew. They were field workers, just like the rest of us, and their lives were no more glamorous than ours, but thanks to the power of their imagination, they created something special for themselves, and I was witness to it.

Nowadays it may be difficult to visualize the friendship and tenderness I saw in their small frame shotgun house, snuggled between two other houses on a tiny odd-shaped lot—but it was there. We were told that Mr. George Stanley's parents were pure-blood Africans. And so it seemed, for he was tall, very dark, and chiseled. Miss Josephine, his wife, was just the opposite. High yellow and petite, she spoke in a very small voice. George Stanley was a gentleman, although no one called him that. People just said, "Ol' Stanley takes care of his woman." And that's exactly what he did. He and Miss Josephine had a unique way of living among us and letting us in on their joy, although as a child I wasn't as concerned about their joy as I was about getting the chance to run behind their car—which doesn't sound exciting, but it was to us young boys. Running behind slow-moving automobiles was one of the games we played. Mr. Stanley drove more slowly than most, and it never seemed to bother him that we were tagging along, keeping up, and patting the shiny black trunk.

What I remember most was his and Miss Josephine's routine, which never changed. While I watched from behind the chinaberry tree, he would always be the first to come out of the house. Then Miss Josephine would come out, lock the door, and walk to the car, where he stood waiting to open the door for her. "Thank you, Mr. Stanley," she would say as she slid into the comfortable backseat. He would then go around to the driver's side, climb in, and away they'd go, laughing and talking back and forth. Mutual admiration flourished in the safety of their car, though segregation hedged them all around. They were the best of friends.

I also saw friendship practiced each time Blind Berta came to town. She always ended up staying with Miss

Shugg Payne, who lived down below the colored school, but somehow everyone seemed to be on notice that she was coming to stay a spell. She had no Seeing Eye dog, only a crooked cane that always tapped along in front of her, but it didn't matter. The entire colored community had special stops along the way to accommodate their friend. Her visits gave them a chance to show their affection. The best food would be cooked, the meat finely chopped, and Blind Berta would be carefully situated on each front porch, eating, laughing, and talking—just as all friends do. I don't know where this lady called home, but every year she would appear, regular as clockwork. For the longest time I thought "Blind Berta" was her name, not a description of her lot in life. If she ever felt lost or alone, her laughter never let on, and the people's friendship seemed to be her vision.

Friendship is the habit of the heart that is probably the easiest for young people to develop, for they can find it among their peers. But as the challenges of life grow more complex—losing loved ones, struggling with illness, trying to make ends meet—friendship must be there also to penetrate the walls that spring up around our sorrows. In a world where loneliness haunts our lives and low self-esteem invades our hearts, it is friendship—when shown and

See next page

shared in the classrooms, in our homes, on the playing
fields, and in the offices where we work—that makes
community real.

Friendship lived in our small community and often
rose to fill occasions that threatened to bring despair.
Today I worry about homeless children and find it difficult to understand how such a precious commodity
could be left unprotected. This haunts me all the more
because I lived among adults who made it a point not to
let their children down. When Miss Lottie Watson was
dying, everyone in town knew that her husband, Charlie,
wouldn't be able to take of their young children by himself. So before Miss Lottie died, friends—most of whom
were not her kin—promised her that she could go in
peace because they would find ways among themselves to
take her children in.

She worried especially about her little girl, Lottie
Jean, whose long black hair was always neatly braided.
But there was no need to fear, because Cousin Beauty, a
prominent member of the community, took Lottie Jean
home and reared her as her own. And Mr. Will and Miss
Henrietta took little Charlie to live with them and their
grandchildren. Their large, rambling house also served
as a barbershop, where the old clippers cut hair and bits
of scalp. When I would go to get my dreaded haircut, I
would see little Charlie playing there among the rest, at
home. There were no orphanages, but it didn't matter.

We had responsible adults practicing friendship among themselves. Today other lives are made better because Lottie Jean is now a registered nurse, living in New York. All of this happened so long ago, and so quietly. It all seemed natural to me.

I needed friendship as a child and our communities will need it tomorrow. Young children laughing and running in day care centers and on playgrounds today will look to us to build a good community for them. And if they are to pass the gift of friendship on, they must see it being practiced. Though our grandchildren may one day have playgrounds on the moon and attend special schools among the stars, laughter and sharing, the evidence of friendship, will still look and sound the same.

THE
FIFTH HABIT
OF THE HEART:
BROTHERHOOD

Within the community, brotherhood is the habit that reaches beyond comfortable relationships to extend a welcome to those who may be different from yourself.

Brotherhood, the far-reaching exten-
sion of friendship, is critical to a world
in which technology brings strangers
into our lives daily. But it is especially
important as we witness the formation of communities
whose only common ground is the desire to assert their
superiority over others. Bound together by fear, mistrust, and misplaced pride, such groups are often vali-
dated by signatures written in other people's blood.
Afraid to face a world where time, space, and respect
must be shared, they hold their "town hall" meetings in
fields, hiding their faces under sheets, their agenda un-
changed since my boyhood days. Or they gather at ral-
lies, finding strength in numbers for their angry,
hate-filled cries. Some shave their heads as an act of
bravado and an impoverished attempt to find "community" somewhere, no matter how disconnected they may
be from real friendships. Some take up arms, forming
isolated enclaves where paranoia about the government
and their fellow citizens becomes their daily bread. The
arms of brotherhood must be long and strong indeed to
reach all the places where healing is required, but this

universal need can be met only if we first reach out to each other right where we live.

The gift of brotherhood will be especially significant to my son and his friends because they have already entered a global community where they are challenged to reach beyond the comfort of their closest relationships to welcome others different from themselves. Their experiences are already being shaped by people who come from different ethnic backgrounds. However, I know that outside their schools there exists the real world where fear, biases, and prejudice still live, waiting to be healed by brotherhood.

I have seen brotherhood before. It found a place in our lives in Glen Allan, in spite of its enemies—legal segregation, racism, and fear. It was brotherhood's impact on my immediate world that assured for me its value as a habit to cultivate and pass on.

In the 1950's the social structure between whites and blacks seemed to be carved in stone. Everyone knew what to expect, and nearly everyone practiced the rules, which had been passed down for generations. Nevertheless, there were still those who reached beyond their comfortable traditional relationships and practiced brotherhood.

I especially recall the stir in Glen Allan when Mr. Freid, a Jewish merchant, hired Miss Maxey, a colored schoolteacher, to work part-time in his store serving both whites and coloreds. Many people now might think, So what? But at the time this was far from an acceptable practice. Mr. Freid's store was big, with large plate-glass windows and huge ceiling fans that evoked the feel of New Orleans. It was our general department store. Hardware and dry goods, nails and dresses, fertilizer and underwear were all there, strategically placed in separate sections. The floor was hardwood, spotless, and seemed to have been oiled daily. But there was only one long counter with one cash register to serve the entire store. We all had to meet at the same spot to pay. And as long as I could remember, only Mr. Freid or his mother had worked the cash register.

Hiring Miss Maxey stirred things up. This just wasn't done, giving a colored person a job up front, with the charge to handle money and wait on both coloreds and whites. It was a small break in our rigid social structure, but it gave some members of the white community of-fense. The colored community was pleased, because we knew Miss Maxey to be as smart as anyone. Yet it was hard for many whites to acknowledge that, for their belief in her inferiority was based on lies that they had come to cherish as fact.

Still, Miss Maxey's hiring wasn't the first of its kind in Glen Allan. Years earlier Mr. Youngblood, another Jewish merchant who had owned a department store in town, had hired Miss Hester Rucker to help him out, when hiring black people into a job reserved for whites was never done. But then the Jews in our community had suffered their own slights, and thus were apt to come down on the side of justice when they had the chance. The Freids, like Mr. Youngblood, practiced brother-hood to the extent they could within our system. Miss Maxey worked there for only a short time, but as long as she did, it was she who rang up the penny nails and the materials for farming.

I also recall the relationship that existed between the senior Mrs. Freid and her colored cook, the same Miss Hester who had worked in Mr. Youngblood's store when she was young. Glen Allan was a town of maids, my mother being one of them, and they all worked hard. Miss Hester, however, displayed a special attitude to-ward her job. I still remember the way she held up her head and the respectful way that she and Mrs. Freid spoke to each other. Not only did Miss Hester hold her head high, but she also admonished the colored kids never to look down, telling us, "There's no need to count the rocks!"

During pecan season Mrs. Freid would graciously let us kids pick as many pecans as we wished from her yard.

Dear Abby

ABIGAIL VAN BUREN

Overeaters find support they need among peers

Dear Abby: The rules for dieting during the holidays you printed prompts this letter. I want to tell you and your readers about my weight loss and recovery from compulsive overeating through Overeaters Anonymous.

Before I found OA at age 19, I had failed at every diet I tried. I wasn't able to stop shoving food down my throat. Back then, I could easily consume eight candy bars, a pint of ice cream and half a pizza in one sitting — then wait for the food to digest so I could go back for more. My emotional state, as you might imagine, was equally tortured. I had suicidal thoughts.

Luckily I found OA which, as many know, is based on Alcoholics Anonymous and has a spiritual component. I walked into my first meeting a confirmed atheist, but I was so desperate that I was ready to try anything. And it worked!

I lost 45 pounds, Abby, but more important, I have kept it off for more than 18 years. One of my closest friends lost 102 pounds through OA and has kept it off for nearly two years. My sponsor, who guides me through the program, lost 250 pounds and has kept it off for 27 years. I'm not making that up.

Incredibly, I don't miss the foods I used to wolf down. I eat nothing sweeter than fresh fruit, and I haven't been plagued by the relentless cravings I used to suffer. OA changed the way I relate emotionally to

(Postage is included in price.)
and IL, P.O. Box 447, Mt. Morris, IL 61054-0447.
let ($4.50 each in Canada) to: Dear Abby Cookbooklets I
envelope, plus check or money order for $3.95 per book-
Recipes." To order, send a business-size, self-addressed

had died as a result of sniffing Pam. I decided to try that, hoping it would kill me. I huffed a number of other aerosol products too. I tried to kill myself by taking an overdose of aspirin. After the second overdose, a friend began dragging me along to activities and focused my attention on other things. My depression lifted, and I finished high school near the top of my class.

A couple of years later depression set in again. I began huffing glue again. I huffed myself into unconsciousness and even a couple of seizures. Paranoia and hallucinations became the norm. The police were called when I was found running around with a knife, sure someone was out to get me. I was hospitalized on at least three occasions.

Fast-forward 20 years: What do I have to show for my stupidity today? I stutter, and confuse similar-sounding words in conversation. My hands shake. I frequently have problems remembering things for

your children and their behavior. Have your children taken an unusual interest in being alone? Does their breath, clothes or room smell funny? Do they have balance problems while walking? Difficulty sleeping? No appetite? Paranoia? Grades falling? ? Personal hygiene lacking? Do you find plastic bags with strange-looking dried-up white stuff in them? Your children could be abusing glue or aerosol products!

Get them help — and don't take "no" for an answer. Abusing household products is as dangerous as abusing illegal drugs.

Senseless in Seattle

Dear Senseless: You may never know how many people you have helped today by giving such a graphic warning to teens and their parents. Your letter is unmistakable proof that substance abuse may mask an even deeper problem, and a caring, tuned-in parent should not minimize or ignore it.

While others would shoo us away, she never did. She always acknowledged our presence and spoke to us, and Miss Hester, her cook, never seemed nervous or bothered that we were there. One day, after spending all morning picking up as many pecans as I could, I was very hungry. But I was uptown and not in the colored section where I lived. Miss Hester, though, seemed to know when my stomach began tightening and talking, which happened as the aroma of her good cooking invaded the yard. The more intense the smell, the closer to the kitchen I picked. Finally Miss Hester came to the door and asked if I was hungry. Of course I was, but I should have said no, as I had been taught. Yet the equality that existed in that house allowed me to say yes. Because Miss Hester felt comfortable asking me in to eat, I had no problem about dropping my task and walking in.

The Jewish families were still somewhat of an oddity in our small community, and we had been taught to look upon their eating habits as somehow mysterious and ungodly. Of course, we were the ones who ate every piece of pork available, which was clearly prohibited by the Old Testament that the entire community embraced. However, rumors of ungodliness were soon dispelled by Miss Hester, who had learned to be a kosher cook—producing stuffed cabbage rolls, a meat dish called kreplach, potato knishes, and other foods that gave off exotic smells.

Often she gave me a sandwich of spicy salami spread with brown mustard, a taste I still recall. She also wanted me to eat matzoh ball soup, but I found the pale, spongy matzoh ball in its pool of broth unexciting next to a salami sandwich and her angel food cake. Because of the brotherhood of mutual respect that was practiced in that house, I was able to pick pecans and also enjoy a snack in a house on the white side of town. Miss Hester and Mrs. Freid built community in front of me and I'll always remember how it tasted, looked, and felt.

Dr. Mary Hogan and Nurse Callie Mae were Glen Allan's health professionals. One white and the other black, they worked as a team. They took care of the sick and delivered the babies, often going into less than desirable dwellings to attend to all kinds of people's needs; but I never heard a colored person in our town speak ill of our doctor or say that she had two standards of treatment. When called, Dr. Hogan and Nurse Callie Mae both came. Their names were always said together and the service they delivered was always welcomed. Working together, they healed the sick, but now I know that what they showed me also fed my soul.

Even though our educational system was legally segregated, a wonderful relationship nonetheless developed between Dr. Norma C. O'Bannon and Mrs. Ann Britton, the supervising educators for Washington County,

Mississippi. Dr. O'Bannon was white and the super-intendent. Mrs. Britton was the supervisor of the colored teachers. I remember them as a team, riding side by side as they came from Greenville to our small town. I am sure they spent their time together on the road, in gentle defiance of the social mores of our day, discussing teaching and our welfare as well as other challenges that faced our principal, Mr. Moore.

Like most students, we looked for ways not to be studying. The visits these ladies paid to our school gave us that, but they gave us more besides. It was rare to see a black woman and a white one dressed equally well and working together as professionals, but they did. They would barely have parked out front when you'd hear Mr. Powell, our janitor, announce that they had arrived. "Hey, y'all!" the welcome cry would come. "Here come Miss O'Bannon and Miss Ann!" And then he would proudly hold the door to let them in. Mrs. Britton's title—Miss Ann—recognized that she was one of us. But both ladies were welcomed, moving from classroom to classroom to deliver short motivational talks, always reminding us that persistence would pay off. They taught by example; after all, both Dr. O'Bannon and Mrs. Britton had reached high and had seized the same professional star.

 Brotherhood is such a powerful habit of the heart that even when only one person reaches out to do right, the impact can be lifelong. If I had not encountered this habit of the heart when I was young, I could have left the South embittered and hurt. Instead I left with purpose and a plan. I could not have done so without the memory of these acts of brotherhood. I needed to see them practiced in front of me to believe that they could happen.

We need this habit today to fall like cleansing rain upon the charred remains of crosses burned in front of synagogues and of churches destroyed by hate. Brotherhood must be continually embraced to rid our communities of racial divisiveness and our homes of dinnertime conversations that put down people who are different from us. We cannot continue as if we have learned nothing from our teacher, the past. And if those around us do not stand shoulder to shoulder for brotherhood, we as individuals must say: I'll do what is right myself, even if no one else will join me. And then we must find others who will stand with us until the rightness of our stance is recognized.

Brotherhood, to be preserved, must be practiced. A good community cannot exist without it.

THE
SIXTH HABIT
OF THE HEART:
HIGH
EXPECTATIONS

*Within the community, high expectations
involve believing that others can
be successful, telling them so, and
praising their accomplishments.*

High expectations were commonplace in our community. They fueled all our dreams. They were bigger than all of us, a collective dream worked out individually. The adults of our community told us daily that we were of value and that big things were expected of us. Even now I feel compelled to do my best—not just for the people I encounter each day, but also for those foundational people who believed in me when no one else did. In spite of legal segregation, racism, and poverty, they believed in their children and also in themselves. They took a giant spiritual leap into a world we could not see but that they knew awaited us. They said we were marked for good, and I believed them.

I still recall their excitement whenever one of their own achieved. They shared the success and passed it on. They taught me the value of being excited at the success of others. I also realized that bearing witness to others' success had to be more than silent observation. We had to let the word out. We had to let others know that we expected them to do well all along, and we could hardly wait to congratulate them on a job well done.

The impact of recognizing and extolling the success of others cannot be overemphasized. In Glen Allan it included being as proud of the day workers' diligence in the fields as we were of our students' good grades. In every case, high expectations were necessary and heartfelt.

High expectations are appropriate to every setting, no matter how sophisticated, but I found them to be especially life-giving during the challenging times we faced as a colored community in the Mississippi Delta. I recall that while picking cotton and sweating unmercifully, the old field hands would talk among themselves about how well the colored farmers were doing in nearby Valewood, which had an independent colored farming community within its borders. Most of the Valewood farmers—many of whom were our friends and members of our extended families—owned their own land, and the day workers in Glen Allan always expected much of them.

They would come to town on Saturdays, and you could always sense Saturday on its way. The smells and sounds of the weekend started around six o'clock on Friday, as whiffs of frying catfish and perch would mingle with the sound of beer tops popping and number three tubs being rinsed out for baths. Tiredness would start loosening its grip and limbs yearning to dance would start to limber up. Then, next morning, we would hear the sound of the trucks and old cars coming in from

Valewood. Every Saturday morning the small uptown area would be lined with colored men, old and young, waiting as they had for years to greet the black farmers when they came to town. Everyone knew the landowners from Valewood. The Buss Lewises, the Duffins, the Brinsons, and scores of others.

Mr. Percy Brinson and his wife and their pickup always arrived midmorning. Although one of his legs had been broken and then bowed out when it healed, Mr. Brinson walked, dressed, and talked the success that many of us knew could also be ours. He was a good farmer and we all rejoiced when his crops came in as planned. Everyone, white and colored, knew him and he knew all of us. With his hat slightly pulled down so that it almost covered one eye, his ever-present cigar, and his neatly dressed wife by his side, he made us realize that not only could we work the fields of others; we might also one day tend our own.

In spite of the setbacks they often faced, many of the black farmers from Valewood enjoyed the same kind of success as Mr. Brinson. It would have been easy to envy those farmers. They owned large tracts of land and for the most part were not beholden to the white landowners. They walked with dignity and carried themselves with pride. But then they were expected to bring in good crops, and when they did, I saw their friends praise their success—a generosity of spirit that served Glen Allan's colored people well.

In a world where the system was rigged against us and our abilities were questioned daily, there was tremendous need for the adults of our community to have high expectations for each other. It was equally important for them to applaud each other's successes. If a community is to be viable, then all of its citizens must be encouraged to maximize their gifts.

Mr. Clarence Hall, Sr., fixed our shoes. Mr. Maxey built our houses. Mr. Will cut our hair. Mr. Walter took us to the fields. Miss Maxey taught us to read and write, do sums, and think. And Miss Callie Mae nursed us back to health. These were but a few of the adults of my small town who managed to create high expectations among themselves. They were challenged by their neighbors to be top-notch, and all received accolades over the years as they created a sense of self-reliance within our community.

Miss Callie Mae lived in the community with her husband, Mr. Bootnanny. Having her there was like having our own private nurse. A short, dark-skinned woman with a ringing voice, Miss Callie Mae was just as good as the doctor to the old people who knew her. A path was beaten to her door by generations of children sent to summon her from her shotgun house. She would always come when called, and when she walked into a home, calm entered with her. Everyone was proud of her and regularly told her so. "Gal, I sho know'd you'd get here," always greeted her.

Although she was Dr. Mary Hogan's nurse, she was our doctor. "Dr. Hogan is blessed to have you working wid her. If'n you'd been white, you'd been gone, but you sticking it out. And we sho need you." She never responded to their praise. She just did her job. Sometimes, while sitting on the sides of old quilt-covered iron beds, she'd hear their thoughts: "Dr. Hogan took my temperature last time. I know it ain't that high. She ain't hold that 'momenther right. She thought I couldn't see her. I could tell. You go on take it. Bless you, honey."

It must have made Miss Callie Mae feel good to see how much she was trusted. I am not sure if she had a degree, but she did have a white dress and cap, which stood out against her ebony skin and dancing eyes. She was expected to be good, and she was.

"He's a builder." That's how we knew Mr. Joe Maxey. On weekends we would see him dressed up, suspenders in place, highly polished shoes, and his seasonal hat—straw in summer, felt in the cooler months. Always talking about politics, voting, and how we young people must go on to high school and college. On weekdays he could be seen in overalls, climbing the walls of partially framed houses, nailing on roofs and siding. If we had our version of an industrialist, it was Mr. Maxey. People worked for him. He worked for himself.

In addition to building houses, he also owned a free-standing barbershop where the colored boys and men of Glen Allan would go to get trimmed and shaved. There were other men in Glen Allan who cut hair, all of them good, but Mr. Maxey made a business out of barbering. Although I also got my hair cut in Mr. Will's kitchen, sometimes my mother or an older relative would take me to Mr. Maxey's, where I waited my turn with other customers to sit in his barber's chair. As we waited, we would encounter men of the town walking out with great pride after a rousing conversation and a good haircut at Mr. Maxey's place, which they cherished as an inde-pendent business. He treated them well. They supported his success and he theirs. Sometimes as an older adult would leave, we young people would get a pat on the head and a question: "You Elder Young's grand, ain't you?" "Yes, sir," I would say. "Thought so," would come the response. "We 'specting good things from you."

Mr. Maxey's success rubbed off on all of us. People remarked that he spoke with a "lifted tongue," which meant to us the sound of strength, independence, and pride conveyed by a person's voice—the clarity of the sound, the careful pronunciation and clear enunciation of one's words, and the ring of expectancy. Deacon

Maxey, as he was called by most of the adults, lived up to our expectations of him. He was more than a house builder and a barber. He also built community.

If the adults expected the best from each other, they expected even more from my generation. Because they had no place of prestige or power from which to proclaim their visions for the future, their often wobbly front porches became that place. Their children, grandchildren, and great-grandchildren became their reasons to strive for excellence, regardless of the obstacles they faced. I recall many conversations that showed them to be a great people full of great dreams for us. Ice cream, homemade vanilla served on Poppa's front porch, provided just another excuse to get together and talk. Between Poppa and my Aunt Willie Mae, we'd have all the fixings needed for a good time. The guests would come, bringing their children and grandchildren along. While we shot marbles or played under the tall house, we could hear them talking about tomorrow, talking about their children who had gone up north or off to college. Though field work was our way of life, their conversations were about a better way of living.

"Where is Ponk's boy, Sidney?" "Well, he's off in Illinois, working on another degree." "Ain't that boy tired of school? Once Ponk put him in, he ain't looked back once!" "Dat Cliff's gonna be jest like him. He ain't much on hard work. I told Ponk the other day that she sho better head him toward the books." "Dey need dat, you know. Thangs are slowly happening down here, yessir. Gonna need dar brains. Dey got good ones, I tell you. 'Fessor White could sho pick um!" They talked, we heard. While we shot marbles, they were shaping our futures. And as they got up to leave, they would pat us on the head and say, "You be your best, now."

Report cards meant as much to the adults in the community as to the children who received them. The whole town knew when it was report card day, and you were expected to parade your good grades so that all the adults could see them. I would even go to the juke joints to show them off. There, amid the wailing of the blues, the men and women of the evening encouraged us to do our best. Though they had limited education, they expected A's from us, and at James Gatson's Café on report card day the men and women gathered to see how each child had done. As Muddy Waters's version of the blues poured forth from the Seeburg jukebox in the bar, we would hand them our well-worn cards. We couldn't wait to show them how well we had done.

And then there was the standard set by Uncle Cleve. "Cleve can do it!" people would exclaim. "If Cleve can't do it, can't be done. Cleve got books. He sent off for 'em. He ain't just gonna scratch his head and tinker, he knows dem cars. Shucks, all the white folk brang dem big cars to him. They like to see 'em open dem books and mumble while he works."

In addition to being the iceman, my Uncle Cleve was the best mechanic around for the high-dollar cars. He had a reputation among both whites and blacks. From Packards to Duesenbergs, Uncle Cleve with his ever-present manuals knew what to do with them. He valued knowledge and always told us that no one could take our knowledge away. Although his schooling was almost nonexistent, he continued to educate himself. His reading and knowledge of the world beyond Glen Allan served him well, just as it served those who watched and admired him. His son, Joe, and I were two of those people. We were proud of his success, and he told us often that whatever he achieved as an entrepreneur, he was doing for us.

When the men of the town, both white and black, brought him their hard-to-solve mechanical problems, he always fixed them. They'd shake their heads and he would just keep on doing what he did best. Uncle Cleve lived for the future. He never spent much time talking about the hurt of segregation. He was motivated by our people who admired him and by the white farmers who trusted him, and he made us know that we must set our own high standards and live by them.

Expecting the best of others and praising their achievements was not just the long-ago practice of a small-town group of visionaries. It must be practiced wherever we live, where we work and where we play. We must look for ways to lift the sights of those who feel downcast, and we must remember to extend words of encouragement and praise when fellow workers, students, volunteers, or teammates have done well.

This is especially important if the accomplishment seems modest but contributes to the building of a good, productive community. Small acts of community-building can be of immense value. For example, I remember, during the voter registration drives of the early 1960's, the talk about the plan to care for the children of the share-croppers. The plan was simply to provide at least one hot meal to their young children. This seemingly small concern and accommodation over the years would lead to a comprehensive program in the Mississippi Delta, one we now know as Project Head Start.

Part of the essential fabric of community is having high expectations for each other. We needed them in Glen Allan when I was growing up. And all of us need them now.

THE
SEVENTH HABIT
OF THE HEART:
COURAGE

*Within the community, courage is standing
up and doing the right thing, speaking out
on behalf of others, and making a commitment
to excellence in the face of adversity
or the absence of support.*

To follow your own code of honor, to sidestep the crowd and do the right thing, and to dream about tomorrow when sometimes just living out your day seems to take everything you have—all of these acts take courage. Throughout the small towns of the South when I was growing up, courage had its place. It was a wonderful tapestry woven with threads of strength, love, and faith in tomorrow.

 I was too young to know Ma Ponk's God, but I was old enough to see her live out her faith. As far as my memory takes me, I can vividly recall the sight of a graying middle-aged lady, after the work of the day was done, fixing her humble meal, boiling her bath water in the iron kettle so she could cleanse her body of the dirt and dust that always accompanied field work, and preparing for bed. This was her ritual, part of her life, and as the night closed the door on daylight, I also saw the rituals of her faith.

The routine of her day was not unlike that of countless thousands of other southern blacks who continued to believe in the future in spite of a world that tried to keep them emotionally shackled to the past. At night, however, after her day was done, she would stand, stretch, and look to the ceiling as if we had family living there. I would watch in awe as the small room opened up to a relationship that was personally hers. Cleaned up, her hair combed for the night, she would turn down the spread, the quilt, and the worn blanket. She was now ready for bed and rest, but not quite. Without saying much to me, she'd kneel at the head of the bed and I would watch her talk to a friend I couldn't see but who was obviously someone she knew well. She never told me to, but I would do the same—kneel, fold my hands, and close my eyes. Afterward she would simply say, "To-morrow gonna be just fine."

It took courage to live day to day in a world that had forgotten she was its sister. Her faith, though, and the rituals she practiced, somehow gave her the assurance she needed to carry on. Every night for the twelve years that I lived at her house, I saw this aging lady feed her courage with a faith that she passed on to me. It continues to serve me well.

If Ma Ponk and the others showed me a courage woven of strength, love, and faith, that tapestry also included a sturdy thread of patience, because life was very hard and the future was never clear. So pervasive and commonplace was my elders' courage that I enjoyed its fruits as a child without ever quite knowing its price.

Most of my life I had been protected by Poppa Young, my great-grandfather, who had reared me, and later on by Ma Ponk, my great-aunt, but I will never forget the day when Mary, my natural mother, was also there for me. I was born out of wedlock when she was very young, but by the time I was thirteen and living with Ma Ponk, my mother, her husband, and my sisters and brother had moved into a house across the road from us, where I ate my meals each day. One day we were surprised to see the white postmistress driving slowly down our road and stopping in front of my mother's house.

White women were rarely seen driving in our small colored community between midmorning and midafternoon, although they were a common sight in the early morning and late afternoon, picking up and dropping off their domestic help. However, this was early afternoon, and as soon as the postmistress stopped, my mother went out to the car, as was the accepted custom. I followed close behind and listened as they talked, and I never forgot the conversation. "Mary, someone stole fifty cents from the post office counter, and your boy was in to pick up mail for y'all."

I was stunned to realized that she considered me the likely thief. But although my mother was visibly shaken, she didn't lack the courage to ask me on the spot if I had taken the money. "I did not," I said, which may not have been the answer the postmistress wanted, but it was the truth. Although I was too young to fully grasp its implications, her accusation hurt. But that hurt was salved as my tall young mother rose to her full height and stood with me, protecting the integrity of my word. It must have been the honesty in my voice and my mother's steadfastness that convinced the postmistress. She just looked at the both of us standing by the rosebush and drove off.

My mother knew that false accusations based on bias and ignorance must always be stopped. But it took courage in that society, and it takes courage now to stand up for what is right. The price extracted for holding one's ground is sometimes high, but if we are to build good community in the presence of others, we must be courageous.

Among others I knew who suffered real pain and paid a real price were the black men who had fought in World War II and the Korean War. Although military heroes are revered in the South, never did these men receive the public recognition they so richly deserved. Yet once their backs had been strong and their eyes had sparkled as they marched off to war. From the plantations they had gone to take their places and show their courage among the ranks of white Americans. They weren't welcomed. But they were needed. Many served. And some died. The others, honorably discharged, came home.

I recall seeing them perched on orange crates and leaning over worn-out domino boards, when, as a child, I paused to hear their stories on my way to the store. They had faced America's enemies abroad and racism at home, and courage had kept their pride intact. They received their small pension checks with humble thanks, and we remembered and honored their legacy. After all, they were American soldiers. In my family Grandpa Shank had served, and when he died, the flag he had for years kept carefully folded in his "shiffro," as he called his wardrobe, was brought home to my mother's house and placed on a shelf where the family's best things were kept. Courage can be memorialized in marble and stone, or it can be kept alive by those who live by its creed, and pass it on.

Poppa Young, whose wisdom and strength of character sustained our family, was a beloved minister in our small community. Even though he was called "Elder" by some, there were those who saw only his color and called him "boy," never giving themselves the opportunity to know his wisdom. I watched Poppa day after day bravely walk out of our home to the outside world whose aim, it seemed, was to keep him down. Though he was called "boy," he kept doing the things that made him "Poppa" to us. He never stooped to their level. It took courage to keep his head held high and his feet straight on the path, but he did, and he made sure to send me on to school where my own path steadily unfolded.

Then there was Mr. Moore, our principal, who once laid his career on the line by insisting that our school get new textbooks when the white schools did instead of the ragged used books full of white children's scribbles and notes that we were usually given. Nor will I ever forget the Hiltons, white storekeepers in Glen Allan, for whom I sacked groceries for nearly four years. Giving me that meager job in their store required courage on their part. Tradition called for a young white boy, not me. But they hired me anyway, which marked a significant change in the way our community looked at things. It was a situation in which the Hiltons chose to do what was right, not just what was convenient and acceptable, and for a while it took courage on my part to do a good job.

Proud as I was of that job, I was also afraid at first. How would the white customers react? What if one of the white farmers insisted his son should have the job? The cotton fields had been a comfortable place for me, although I had also longed to leave. This job brought me inside, out of the blazing sun and into the coolness of southern ceiling fans—a different world for me, one where I would readily adapt as I followed the habits practiced by Poppa, Uncle Cleve, and Ma Ponk.

 Our society still struggles to find the courage to do what is right and to build humane communities where all of us can live. Issues of race that our great-grandparents faced have not been resolved. Every so often we stand together, but eventually something happens between the races that causes us to run to our historical points of reference. From the highly charged trial of the Los Angeles police officers accused of beating black motorist Rodney King to the tragic example of Susan Smith, who fabricated a black carjacker to explain the disappearance of her little boys whom she herself had drowned, we deal with the wedge of "color" that keeps us from focusing on what is right and wrong, evil and good. It takes courage to look beyond other people's color and ethnic origins and deal together with the real culprits, whose attitudes and actions seek to destroy the Habits of the Heart.

In the 1960's, when the civil rights movement came to our town, many people who were thought to be Uncle Toms and uncommitted surprised everyone by flexing muscles of strength and determination. Fueled by the witness and example of Martin Luther King, Jr., and emboldened by the civil rights policies of the Kennedy administration, many people in our community joined in the spirit of the Mississippi Delta sharecropper Fannie Lou Hamer, who declared that once she stood up, she would never bow again.

Miss Hamer had earned the right to make her bold declaration. From the fields of the Delta she brought to the nation a strength and courage that still serve as an example to us all when giving up may seem to be the best way out. Jailed and beaten, threatened with loss of home and life, this lady became a modern-day Sojourner Truth as she declared to the world her need to participate in the government of our nation, which she claimed as her God-given right. Miss Hamer helped the black people of Mississippi to register to vote and shook up politics in her home state and nationwide.

Not all those who joined the movement were black, nor were they all old and gray. As the movement progressed, there was such a cry for equality that young people of all races could be found among the committed and the caring. Young black girls and boys were learning at an early age that the freedom they had been taught about would come at a price. And so they learned new things: how to march, how to chant, and how not to be afraid.

It took courage to join a movement that had stirred the antipathy of the Ku Klux Klan and claimed the lives of people in bombings, lynchings, and rifle fire. Nevertheless, in Mississippi, as in other segregated states of the deep South, civil rights workers of every age and condition carried on, refusing to flinch in the face of violence and contempt. During those struggling civil rights years, youthful innocence was lost, but a model of courage was etched in people's souls.

Courage has many faces, speaks a thousand languages, and lives all over the world, but I believe it looks the same to everyone. Courage is still needed to battle the enemies that seek to destroy our communities—racism, for example, which shows up everywhere, whether its object is the "ethnic cleansing" of the Bosnians, the slaughter of nomadic Kurds, or the demoralization of black and interracial communities by burning their churches down.

Indeed, community-building and community-saving require many different kinds of courage—regardless of whether the community is the town or city where you live, the school you attend, your place of worship, your social club or professional organization, or your workplace. It takes courage to stand up to the person who spreads false stories about you; to the boss who demands favors in exchange for a raise; or to the fellow student who plagiarizes your work. It takes courage just to keep doing what you're supposed to do every day when the returns seem small but others are counting on you. And it also takes courage to keep your gaze on what is right when all around you people are padding their expense accounts, deceiving their spouses, or cheating customers, using "everybody's doing it" as their excuse.

Courage always involves risk. Fighting for your country or standing up for social justice can cost you your life. Standing up to the boss can cost you your job. And standing up to your peers can threaten your social standing. But courage also reaps rewards, not only for those who practice it but for those who witness it. For those who practice it, courage always confirms your own value. And when others observe your courage, the whole community is stronger, for other people can draw strength in the midst of their troubles from the example you have set.

I once saw this legend on a coat of arms: Courage grows strong at a wound. Certainly Poppa Joe, Ma Ponk, Mr. Moore, the former soldiers, and many other people in my small town of Glen Allan knew the truth of that. They struggled courageously against the wounding power of racism and the threat of poverty, not by acting like those who tried to keep them down, but by keeping faith with the best that they could be. It is my good fortune to bear witness to their courage and to honor it by practicing as best I can this habit of the heart.

THE
EIGHTH HABIT
OF THE HEART:
HOPE

*Within the community, hope is believing
in tomorrow—because you have
learned to see with your heart.*

When I was growing up, hope was like the good air we breathed. We would not have been able to survive without it. Hope enabled my family and friends to look beyond the present circumstances to an uncertain future. They were able to hold my hands steady, because hope held their hearts. As I grew older, I knew hope to be important because a whole social movement had grown up around the slogan Keep Hope Alive—a cry from urban America to save the lives of urban youth. Hope, immeasurably valuable, cannot be purchased, bartered, or borrowed—it can only be shared and nurtured from heart to heart. And every good community has been built upon it.

Hope awaited me when I was born. It was February of 1945 and the Christmas and New Year's celebrations, which always brought such joy to our community, had just faded from sight. My mother, Mary, was only nineteen, unmarried, and not ready for parenthood, and Mama Pearl was worried about her condition. Prenatal care was unknown to our family, so they could only pray for a healthy delivery. I have been told that the night I was

born my mother's labor pains came quickly and unex-
pectedly, but Miss Lottie Jones, the sage old midwife, had
been alerted and, with the anxious help of Poppa Joe and
Mama Pearl, had turned the small bedroom into a caring
maternity ward. Thus they made ready for my arrival.

Just as they had once welcomed my mother into the
world, they now welcomed me. Many years earlier, after
my mother's parents divorced, Poppa Joe and Mama
Pearl brought her into their home and raised her as their
own. And like my mother, I would be part of their future. Entering a home where people loved me, and later
moving on to live with my great-aunt, I would be nestled
within their community, a place where I would live until
I graduated from high school, drawing from all their
dreams my vision for the future. Within the safety of a
world that Poppa, and later Ma Ponk, helped to craft
and fashion for me, I would grow up to be a man.

But of course that world felt anything but safe to them.
The year I was born, the world was at war, and colored
people in the South were treated as second-class citizens.
The right to vote was not universal and the legacy of slavery could still be seen. The schools were separate and un-
equal and the pay for field work was too meager to allow
anyone to build any kind of family estate. Martin Luther
King, Jr., was in his teens, John and Robert Kennedy
were just young men, and the civil rights movement was

as yet a quiet dream. Old colored men filled with wisdom and knowledge were called "boys," and many of the women who would teach me how to dream could find work only as servants and workers in the fields. The doors of the Glen Allan library were not opened to them, nor would they be open to me, and the front doors of our white neighbors' homes were locked to us. This was my elders' reality, one designed to make them feel inferior, but one that they prayed about and sheltered me from. They were able to do this because of hope.

The schoolteacher, Miss Maxey, and my great-grandmother Mama Pearl conspired to educate me for a world that had not fully welcomed them. Through the eyes of hope they saw a future I could not even imagine. Living surrounded by cotton fields that would exhaust their bodies without ever taxing their brains, they nonetheless embraced education and revered the black educators, many of whom were simply called " 'Fessor."

Although I met him only once, I'll never forget the time that the pioneering 'Fessor White came back to town. He had lived in Glen Allan years before, and had become a legend by my time. A college man himself, he had educated the sons and daughters of nearly all the field hands and had also shown them the value of higher education. With each successful graduate, he had dispelled the rumors of their lack of ability and had made a family proud. None was more proud than Ma Ponk, my great-aunt, because 'Fessor White had both taught and inspired Sidney and Melvin, her boys.

Every time we passed by the white frame school building that sat in the middle of the colored community, Ma Ponk pointed out the big oak tree. " 'Fessor White and my boy Sidney planted that tree. Never thought it'd grow, but 'Fessor White shore thought so." Sidney had gone on to become an educator himself, being the first person in our town to receive a doctoral degree, so I had heard all about this rotund 'Fessor White, and I could hardly wait to meet him. He had been retired for years. He was aging and didn't travel much. When he finally returned to Glen Allan, he was welcomed, fed, and fussed over in every home.

At Ma Ponk's house he was given her chair, the rocker with the cushion. And pleasure shone from his round black face and bright, observant eyes. I sat near them and listened as they laughed and talked about an era long since gone, but always alive to them. I laughed as they recalled Melvin's lack of attention and how irritated it had made the professor. It seemed as if the professor wanted Melvin to learn, learn, learn, and Melvin just wanted to play. Ma Ponk's chest of drawers was just across from where we were sitting. That's where she kept her pictures. I watched as she pulled them out and listened as she proudly told the professor about Sidney's family. As they examined the pictures of his wife, Beatrice, and his daughter, Debra, he turned and looked out the front window at the new brick school that looked so big alongside the white frame building where he had taught.

"Miss Elna," he said to Ma Ponk, "it seems so long ago that I was here. The school seemed much bigger then. There was so much I wanted to do, so many lives I wanted to touch. You know so many of the young ones lived on plantations and just weren't able to get to us. But there were some, parents like you, old man Ayers, and Elder Young, who pushed your kids. I'm so grateful you did. I know it was hard. But I'm glad you did it."

He paused and smiled at her. "I knew your boy Sidney had it in him. He was mischievous but bright. So glad to hear how well he's representing us." And then he nodded toward the window. "Miss Elna, just raise your head a bit, and you'll see the top of that oak tree. Me and your boy and a few others planted it. Do you remember?"

"Sho do, 'Fessor," Ma Ponk responded with a smile. "I thought you was wasting time. Never thought it would give you shade!"

"I know." He nodded. "But look at it now, branching all out everywhere, just like our educated colored boys and girls. A small start, but we haven't seen the end."

They talked on into the afternoon, and their conversation stayed with me. The oak tree is still growing, symbolizing for me the hope that lived in their hearts and lives on in mine.

Educational opportunities in our community far outnumbered business opportunities for us—at least the type that help you get ahead. Yet my Uncle Cleve and Aunt Willie Mae overcame limited schooling to paint for many of us a picture of perseverance that I will always remember. Although they never became real estate tycoons as defined by Wall Street, they certainly became members of our respected "Five Hundred" by the standards of a small colored community in the 1950's.

As a couple they looked to the future and lived a hope that we could all see. Every time a lot came up for sale, they scraped the money together to buy it. They had small lots all over Glen Allan. They were landowners and landlords. Other black people rented from them. Uncle Cleve kept up the property, paid the taxes, and was always looking for a new piece to buy. It was important to me to be able to walk with him as he checked the properties and talked with his tenants. In a world that seemed to have been built on dependence, he showed me independence and hope.

While Uncle Cleve was performing as a businessman and creating a legacy to remember, legislators in the Mississippi House and Senate were still debating old racist agendas that included discussions of black people's intelligence. My elders continued to perform in spite of what those in power thought of them. Even today those agendas exist, but so does the hope that saw us through. Uncle Cleve and his kind worked hard and saved because they believed in providing a strong foundation for their hope.

Uncle Cleve used the bank in Greenville at a time when many of the old people were still afraid to trust the banks or let the white community know just how much money they had managed to save. Behind the henhouses of their small homes, small fortunes were buried, and ready cash was still being stashed under mattresses throughout town. I know, because Ma Ponk kept her operating capital under the mattress, and Cousin Lulu from the colored colony was rumored to have buried her money in iron pots near the henhouse. They saved because they saw a future that I was too young to visualize and they were too wise to ignore.

And though we, their children, toiled alongside them in the fields, Mother Luella Byrd saw a vision of what we could become and set out to direct our paths accordingly. Without access to public buildings, libraries, or professional theater groups, she turned the old St. Mark's Missionary Baptist Church into a stage upon which she brought the arts into our lives. Overweight, stern faced, and with an odd gait that made her seem deformed, Mother Byrd used the altar of the church to lift our sights beyond the fields. She directed great dramas. Everyone came out to see how she could transform their children into voices of history and the future. Because she was very serious, especially about *her* role in our lives, we were sort of scared of her. She would have rehearsals at night, giving us time to get home from the fields. But if we were late, it was not unusual for her to appear on our doorsteps, knocking on the door, and asking our parents why.

Easter was Mother Byrd's big day. She wanted us to shine. Poems would be recited and the resurrection scene reenacted, in which colored children from the Delta became Jewish and Roman citizens of Jesus' time. When we practiced our parts, she stood at the back of the church and, folding her hands behind her back, would bellow, " 'Nounce it correctly!" Because of her hope, an ideal that was practiced among the missionary women she knew, our small world was enlarged. She believed in us. When others asked "Why?" she turned a deaf ear and continued her own mission: to use drama, public speaking, singing, memorizing, and writing to show us a different picture of ourselves.

Mother Byrd could not deliver us from the drudgery of backbreaking field work, but she was determined that it would not blind or break us. Today we need a Mother Byrd in every city and town where drugs and the illicit dollars they earn have blinded our young people's eyes, hardened their hearts, and created a cycle of violence and despair; where young girls trade their futures for a high they think they need to survive, and wake up having given birth to babies they are much too young to mother; and where violent death comes at the hands of brothers who in my day would have pledged their lives to protect each other. Hope still must be the antidote to such despair. We need people willing to become Mother Byrds, knocking on doors at night, challenging parents to be accountable, and enlarging children's expectations of themselves.

Mother Byrd and her kind were wise beyond our understanding. They started their rescue efforts early, long before we knew that we could lose our own way and slip outside the circle of their love. They began their good work when we were just barely able to talk, and they never quit. They never told us that our teenaged years could be terrible. They just practiced the Habits of the Heart continually, involving us in them as if we had no other choice. They taught for life, which for them ended only at the grave. The older they got, the harder they worked. And they continued until they had no life left. Their message was clear: Giving and practicing hope is a job from which we can never retire. And the church was at the center of their work.

I grew up going to church. We dressed up on Sundays and proudly walked into the frame structures that were our places of worship. First it was Poppa Young and Mama Pearl, the preacher and his wife, who always carried me along. Some have said it was the church that kept us under white control because the civility it brought to our world made us docile as well. But the teachings my elders shared seemed always to leave room for humanity to change and mature. And I prefer to believe that rather than letting their faith make them docile, my elders relied on the church to sustain them during the process of social change, of which they continually dreamed. I heard great preachers, uneducated men, who could dig deep into your emotions and give you hope when reality said, "Ain't nothing gonna change." Later when I went to live with my great-aunt, Ma Ponk, who was a respected mother in the church, I was duty-bound never to miss a service. Even when I didn't want to go, seeds of hope were planted there that continue to fuel my life.

Because we weren't allowed to use public meeting places in the town, the church was the center of our spiritual and social life. Men, women, and children, we all went and listened to the sermons that kept the old people's dreams alive while nurturing the visions of the young. We sang the songs that enabled the old and the lame to work just one more day. Within the safety of the church walls, hope welled up and stretched from Sunday to Sunday, and I saw it shared among the adults who built my community.

The world still encounters the truth of Langston Hughes's poem, "Harlem," about dreams deferred: They are likely either to dry up like "raisins in the sun" or to explode. Hughes's words were made famous by Lorraine Hansberry's award-winning play, *A Raisin in the Sun*, which for years made visible the drama of black life and our grappling with a society that failed to recognize our dreams. Dreams still require hope to sustain them—just as hope holds the blocks of community together. The world must never forget how hope looks, acts, and feels, or the obligation each individual has to practice it, share it, and pass it along.

TRANSCENDING
HABITS

Once I gave my speech to the graduating seniors in Illinois, I began to see that the Habits of the Heart were never the private property of the Mississippi Delta or captive to the time in which I saw them employed. I believe that they came into the Delta from somewhere else, looking for hearts to call home before moving on. I first encountered them in Glen Allan, but the adults who built my community had seen them practiced in Louisiana, North Carolina, and Alabama, and even in Europe and Africa. And an encounter in Germany, not long after my talk to the North Shore graduates, showed me that the habits are universal.

I was staying in the quaint town called Bad Kreuznach, which was the perfect place for a writer. The trees of Bad Kreuznach were heavy with secrets I wanted to know, and as I watched older citizens walk hand in hand along the Nahe River, I yearned to speak German so I could talk to them. The words we uttered, trying to communicate, were strange mumblings that required many gestures to complete their meaning. But when our eyes met, our hearts spoke, and we waved, smiled, and seemed to understand. On my first night there, after walking along the river amid lush foliage that enveloped the ancient buildings, I went back to my hotel for dinner.

While sitting in the lobby waiting for my friend and the sponsor of my lecture tour, Betty Nicholas, I was suddenly overrun by what appeared to be a German soccer team. The sweat, the dirt, and the soccer ball gave them away, I thought. Although I didn't feel conspicuous, all of the players nodded, waved, and smiled, which made me wish that I could ask them about their team. Instead I sat and listened to them talk to the hotel clerk.

Finally one of the group broke ranks and walked over to me. "You American?" he asked in English, and I happily said, "Yes." Then, to my surprise and pleasure, I learned that they were not athletes but salesmen in town for an international training conference, and they were staying in my hotel. They were from different countries in Europe, but all could speak at least some English and could help me enjoy this small town. They laughed when I told them I had thought they were professional athletes, from whom I had planned to get autographs for my son. They had just been out playing soccer for fun. Although all were friendly, I seemed to strike a special chord of friendship with two of them, René and George. They stayed behind and talked with me while I waited to go to dinner with my friend, and we made plans to have dinner together the following night.

The next evening, as we settled down to our meal, we talked about our families and our places of birth. All evening both René and George kept apologizing for not being fluent in English, but their English was far better than my German. And the memory of our elders connected us even more as we talked into the night.

I was the first American that René had ever met. He had grown up, fatherless, behind the Berlin Wall in East Germany. But in spite of the hardships under Communist rule, his mother and grandparents had created a nurturing community for him. His *opa*, or grandfather, was the constant man in his life, and in his company he developed a deep love for the quaint village of his birth, its people, and its ancient buildings. Although Communist rule was harsh and there was seldom enough money, his grandparents managed to shield his heart from bitterness, as mine had done for me. Indeed, growing up behind the Berlin Wall, he had encountered many of the same habits of the heart that I had encountered in Glen Allan. His family also showed him a future that he was too young to envision, but they held to the hope that it would be there for him. Even after the wall between East and West Germany was down and René had access to all of Europe, so strong were his ties to the caring adults in his life that he chose not to leave the East. The people he loved were still there and he wanted to be with them. So he had chosen to learn all he could abroad, but to employ that knowledge in the community that had given him life.

René remembered his Opa just as I remembered my Poppa, and George, who was from Croatia, remembered his grandfather. I never thought that I'd be talking to a young man from Croatia, a country that was making the nightly news back home. While we spoke about the on-going war, the ever-increasing casualties, and the devastated countryside, it took me back to the time when I was a young soldier in the air force and the fear of a Vietnam assignment had gripped my heart. Yet here I was sitting down to dinner with a man whose relatives were dying daily, and when he spoke of his family, he spoke of to-morrow. So rich and impressionable were George's early years that even the war could not take away the memory of the dream that had been created for him. As I sat and listened, his conversation turned from the war to his hope for the days after, when it would all be over and he could return home to build his bed-and-breakfast along the Adriatic Sea. That had been his family's dream.

The dream of a good community is universal and so are the habits that build the dream. I see this every time I travel and meet people from all over the world, and it was reinforced recently when I lectured before a group of Russian journalists. They had come to America to explore the role of writers and journalists in furthering the cause of human rights, and I had been asked to address them.

I shared with them the Eight Habits of the Heart, saying that human rights have a prominent place wherever the Habits are practiced. Although we spoke through an interpreter, nothing seemed to be lost in the translation. And I shall never forget the question that Aleksandr Viktorovich Fralov asked about my optimism and basic ideals. He wanted to know the source of my faith in the future, considering that my life had been followed by a cloud of racism. "Aleksandr," I responded, "you are correct in your observation. My life has been shadowed by the menace called racism, but this menace was unable to keep my elders from exercising their responsibility to build a world for me. Had they not valued the Habits of the Heart and nurtured the tiny sapling of hope in me, I would not be here lecturing today."

As I watched Aleksandr and his colleagues nod their heads, I knew that they subscribed to these same ideals. At the close of the lecture Aleksandr embraced me and began to cry, and I shared his embrace, his tears, and his yearning for a better world.

My encounters with René, George, Aleksandr, and many others from around the world reinforced what I already knew—that my life actions are important not only to my son, who watches everything I do and hears what I say, but also to the adults that I encourager, and to their daughters and sons. The Habits cannot be passed along like a collection of footballs. What we are passing along are the strengths of our lives, which we embrace and make clear through daily living.

Adults must earn a living to support our families and ourselves, but in our pursuit of a livelihood, we must never give way to covetousness or greed, lest we model for our children and others an obsession with material things. In families and communities with such a focus, the sick are overlooked, the young are unwanted, and the elderly are set aside.

Building for the future has never been a mechanical pursuit. It has always involved tapping the energies and imaginations of our youth: kids on the streets, the homeless ones as well as those who are well-fed and well-bred. The future also resides with the youth of distant lands, who speak languages we do not know. The start they get in life, and the values they see practiced, will make all the difference in the kinds of communities they build.

Although my personal world was shaped by the indelible imprint of slavery—just as others' worlds have been marked by iron and bamboo curtains, ethnic cleansing, the doctrine of apartheid, and the legacy of tribal mistrust—the will of ordinary folk to work together as my elders did remains the only force that can ensure that good community exists.

Just as the ordinary people of the Mississippi Delta like Poppa Joe, Ma Ponk, Mr. Fields, Mother Byrd, Mrs. Freid, and Cousin Beauty built a good community for me, so must adults and youth live out the principles of good community—the Eight Habits of the Heart— around the globe. The dream of good community is universal, as are the habits that build that dream. Those habits are mobile, vital, and never out of date, and they continually seek among the peoples of the world good hearts in which to dwell.

PASSING ALONG THE EIGHT HABITS OF THE HEART

*Exercises to Prompt
Practice and Reflection*

Passing Along the Eight Habits of the Heart is a series of activities designed to help you practice the Eight Habits by reflecting on your own values and ideals. The exercises are designed for use in small groups: at home among family or friends, at the public library, at church or synagogue, at school, at work, or anywhere that people come together to build community. Each member of the group should have the opportunity to participate in the exercise and share in the discussion.

All that is required is:

- someone to convene the group,
- a commitment to meet at least five times,
- a willingness to read some of the materials listed, and
- a willingness to use the exercises as a process of discovery.

You may wish to use a small notebook for your exercises, which can also function as a Habits of the Heart journal.

These basic activities can become powerful tools when shared in the presence of others. When I use these with groups, emotions often run high; voices crack and tears sometimes appear as memories are unlocked about the significant people in the participants' lives.

The activities remind us that very little in life that's good happens without the presence of one or more of the Eight Habits. However, not all the memories shared will be good ones. That's okay. You can't change the past, but you *can* battle negative habits within your own community.

The goal of the activities is to assist you in personalizing the Eight Habits and applying them to your own life. Please start by listening carefully to the first-person stories of others. You are building community right where you sit.

HABITS OF THE HEART GROUP ACTIVITY I

Good deeds take on human faces in this activity, which involves sharing photographs and memories.

Each participant will need:
 • paper (or a small notebook) and a pencil or pen

- a photograph of a family member or family group, or of a friend or friends—a person or group who has had a positive influence on your life

STEP 1

To begin, write down the first two or three words or phrases that come to your mind when you hear the word *community*. For example, past groups have come up with these phrases:

- "Friends and family"
- "Working together"
- "Sharing good food" (a personal favorite)
- "Children and senior adults sharing time"
- "Bearing each other's emotional crises"

STEP 2

After everyone in the group has finished writing, read your words aloud. Then show your photograph and discuss how the individual(s) in that photo made your life memorable by building community in your presence. This step can call forth a range of emotions from the group as precious photos and unique memories are shared. The words you wrote down in Step 1 can help you to focus on what *community* means to you.

STEP 3

As you discuss the people in your photograph, ask the group to help you list all the habits of the heart that can be recognized from the discussion.

STEP 4

From that list, note the habits that you currently practice as well as the ones that need additional attention. Discuss with the group: How can you adapt those habits practiced by the person or people in your photograph to your own life?

STEP 5

Take two of the habits listed as needing work and write out what you will do for the next month to increase your practice of those habits.

HABITS OF THE HEART GROUP ACTIVITY II

Reading about people who build community in diverse ways stimulates discussion of our own upbringings—and challenges us to practice the Habits of the Heart in our own lives.

Each participant will need:

- paper and pencil or pen
- reading list at the back of this guide

STEP 1

Before the meeting, select and read a piece of literature from the family reading lists that follow these exercises. For longer works, read preselected passages.

STEP 2

Discuss with the group how your reading made you feel and what memories of your own upbringing surfaced. For instance, many participants in groups I have worked with talked about the character of Poppa, my great-grandfather, after reading my book *When We Were Colored.* They identified him with uncles and grandparents who had included them in rituals that helped to shape the adults they would become.

Again, not all memories will be positive. Your group might include comments such as, "This is what I wish my family had been like." That is okay. Remember that you have the power to build community in your life now.

STEP 3

With the group, identify and discuss the habits of the heart that were portrayed in your reading.

STEP 4

From that list, note the habits that you currently practice as well as those that need additional attention.

STEP 5

Of the habits discussed, write down one that you choose to practice more fully in your life.

STEP 6

Decide the action and the time frame that you will need to model the habit chosen. Your reading may give you specific ideas. Write your plans down for reference.

HABITS OF THE HEART GROUP ACTIVITY III

Writing a postcard to someone important in our past sparks a discussion of how we can help to shape the lives of others.

Each participant will need:
- postcard
- pencil or pen

STEP 1

Write an imaginary postcard thanking one person for a specific deed that you feel did the most to help you build your personal emotional community.

STEP 2

After everyone in the group has finished writing, share your postcard with the group. Again, be prepared for visible emotional responses to this activity; the act of writing can unleash a flood of memories.

STEP 3

With the help of the group, decide which habits of the heart were practiced by the recipient of your postcard.

STEP 4

Discuss with the group how you as an individual can implement these habits in your community over the next several months. Many group participants later told me that following this activity, they went home and wrote a letter to a special aunt, uncle, teacher, or coworker "to tell them just how important they were in my life."

HABITS OF THE HEART GROUP ACTIVITY IV

Many participants take this activity as a call to action to try to improve their own community.

Each participant will need:

- paper and pencil or pen

STEP 1

Think of a place, real or imagined, that feels like the *opposite* of a good community to you. On a blank piece of paper, list all the characteristics you associate with that place. One participant, remembering a neighborhood she used to pass through on the way to work, wrote:

- Bars on windows
- Lack of trust, suspicion of strangers
- Litter and vandalism, feeling that people just don't care

STEP 2

When everyone has completed his or her list, discuss with the group a time when you experienced one of these anticommunity traits and how it made you feel. For instance, the above participant told of her anger and sadness when a wall in her own building was vandalized.

STEP 3

Next, on the reverse side of your paper, write down the habits of the heart that could cancel the negative trait you have just described. Friendship and responsibility were the habits that the participant selected to fight vandalism.

STEP 4

Pick one of these habits and discuss how the practice of this habit could have changed the negative situation you described.

STEP 5

Discuss with the group: Do one or more of these negative traits exist within your real community? Decide which negative traits you will focus on as a group, and discuss the habit(s) of the heart that could cancel the situation(s) over a period of time if practiced by everyone.

In the above example, the group's town had a problem with graffiti spray-painted on community walls that had been painted and decorated with great care by the area's children. The group's discussion focused on the habit of responsibility: "Responsibility means caring for the place you live whether you've been there all your life or are just passing through. If everybody does this, your own home and the next place you go are pleasant places to be."

Use your journal to lay out a plan to practice the good habit(s) during the coming months. "The graffiti damage is done," the group concluded, "but we can write letters to the newspaper, talk to the school board, and work with our own youth groups to organize programs that stress respect for our neighborhoods."

HABITS OF THE HEART GROUP ACTIVITY V
Recalling the special things that people have done for us reminds us to help build special memories for others.

stirred her soul and moved her to a higher sense of service, which Edelman views as the very purpose of life.

Frankl, Viktor E. *Man's Search for Meaning: An Introduc-
tion to Logotherapy.* 4th ed. Boston: Beacon Press, 1992
(hardcover); New York: Pocket Books, 1988 (paper).
The inspirational story of psychiatrist Frankl, who was
imprisoned at Auschwitz during World War II. Frankl
outlines the principles of logotherapy and offers ways to
help us focus on finding the purpose in our lives.
Preselected reading: Chapter 2

Peck, M. Scott. *Further Along the Road Less Traveled: The
Unending Journey Toward Spiritual Growth.* New York:
Simon & Schuster, 1993 (hardcover); 1994 (paper). In
a series of essays, psychiatrist Peck shows that the road
we travel is rather like a series of concentric circles ex-
panding out from the core. Addressing the stages of personal and spiritual development, he stresses the
importance of looking to a source greater than ourselves
to make our way and to help each other.
Preselected reading: Chapter 8

Taulbert, Clifton L. *When We Were Colored.* Tulsa, OK:
Council Oak Books, 1989 (as *Once Upon a Time When
We Were Colored,* hardcover); New York: Penguin
Books, 1995 (paper). A coming of age memoir set in the
Mississippi Delta amidst family and friends who form a
ring of protection around young Cliff while nurturing
his dreams.
Preselected readings: Chapters 1, 3, 9, and 11

Taulbert, Clifton L. *The Last Train North*. Tulsa, OK: Council Oak Books, 1992 (hardcover); New York: Penguin Books, 1995 (paper). The story of one naive and hopeful "colored boy" struggling to become the strong, successful black man his southern community has sent him north to be. Sequel to *When We Were Colored*. **Preselected readings: Chapters 6, 8, and 11**

Walker, Alice. *In Love & Trouble: Stories of Black Women*. New York: Harcourt Brace & Company, 1973 (paper). A collection of stories about black women who are struggling with the issues of tradition and modern society. **Preselected reading: "Everyday Use"**

Middle/High School

Barnes, Joyce Annette. *Promise Me the Moon*. New York: Dial Books for Young Readers, 1997. At age thirteen, smart, sassy Annie must decide whether or not she wants to attend an elite high school that will help her pursue her love of science—and take her away from everything that's familiar to her.

Collier, James Lincoln and Christopher Collier. *War Comes to Willy Freeman*. New York: Bantam Doubleday Dell Books for Young Readers, 1987 (hardcover); Yearling Books, 1989 (paper). Readers meet the Arabus family in this first volume in a saga about the life of a black family and their friends during the American Revolution.

Lasky, Kathryn. *Pageant.* New York: Simon & Schuster Children's Books, 1986 (hardcover); Dell, 1988 (paper). Sarah Benjamin is Jewish but attends a private Christian girls' school in Indianapolis in the 1960's. Readers meet her family, friends, and teachers, and see how the events of the sixties affect her life.

L'Engle, Madeleine. *The Arm of the Starfish.* New York: Farrar, Straus & Giroux, 1965 (hardcover); Dell, 1980 (paper). Against the background of a dramatic suspense story, sixteen-year-old Adam learns that science, like love, is a gift to be shared with others.

Lord, Bette Bao. *In the Year of the Boar & Jackie Robinson.* New York: HarperCollins Children's Books, 1984 (hardcover); HarperTrophy, 1986 (paper). Shirley Temple Wong, called Bandit, comes from China in 1947 to live with her father in Brooklyn. Though she knows only a few words of English, playing baseball helps her to feel she is a part of the American Dream.

Taulbert, Clifton L. *When We Were Colored.* Tulsa, OK: Council Oak Books, 1989 (as *Once Upon a Time When We Were Colored,* hardcover); New York: Penguin Books, 1995 (paper). A coming of age memoir set in the Mississippi Delta amidst family and friends who form a ring of protection around young Cliff while nurturing his dreams.

Preselected readings: Chapters 1, 3, 9, and 11

Taulbert, Clifton L. *The Last Train North*. Tulsa, OK: Council Oak Books, 1992 (hardcover); New York: Penguin Books, 1995 (paper). The story of one naive and hopeful "colored boy" struggling to become the strong, successful black man his southern community has sent him north to be. Sequel to *When We Were Colored*. **Preselected readings: Chapters 6, 8, and 11**

Walker, Alice. *In Love & Trouble: Stories of Black Women*. New York: Harcourt Brace & Company, 1973 (paper). A collection of stories about black women who are struggling with the issues of tradition and modern society. **Preselected reading: "Everyday Use"**

Children

Bang, Molly. *The Paper Crane*. New York: Greenwillow Books, 1985 (hardcover); Mulberry, 1987 (paper). In return for a meal, a gentle stranger gives a restaurant owner a magic paper crane, wonderfully repaying the owner's generosity.

Bunting, Eve. *The Wednesday Surprise*. New York: Clarion Books, 1989 (hardcover); 1990 (paper). Preparing an extra-special surprise for Dad's birthday, seven-year-old Anna teaches her grandmother to read.

Coerr, Eleanor. *The Josefina Story Quilt*. New York: HarperCollins Children's Books, 1986 (hardcover);